"The more you give, the more you get. Nowhere is this truer than in business. The companies which are truly devoted to doing good in the world also make a huge positive impact on their business. Rosica offers a compelling argument and clear guidance on turning good deeds into good strategy."

Simon Sinek, author of Start with Why: How Great Leaders Inspire Everyone to Take Action and Leaders Eat Last: Why Some Teams Pull Together and Others Don't

"Rosica is a master at creating strategically smart marketing plans that position entrepreneurs for fast growth."

Verne Harnish, author of *Mastering the Rockefeller Habits: What You Must Do to Increase the Value of Your Fast-growth Firm*

"A wonderful, increasingly enjoyable book. I would recommend it to anyone who loves to be challenged, and even more to anyone who isn't ready for it."

Michael E. Gerber, author of *The E-Myth books*

"Chris Rosica explores one of the most under-utilized techniques in marketing. Well written and convincing."

> **Al Ries,** author of Focus: *The Future of Your Company Depends On It, The 22 Immutable Laws of Marketing,* and *Positioning: The Battle for Your Mind*

"Rosica offers fresh insight into the unspoken emotional needs of the customer. This book shows how taking the time to build a truly authentic brand can deliver lifelong customers and robust profits."

> **Geoff Smart, Ph.D.**, chairman and CEO of ghSMART, co-author of *Topgrading*, and master trainer

The Power of B2B Social Media

*The Marketing Strategy
You Can't Afford to Ignore*

Chris Rosica

NOBLE PRESS

Published by Noble Press
Noble Press
512 Three Mile Harbor/Hog Creek Rd.
East Hampton, NY 11937, U.S.A.

Copies of this book may be purchased at amazon.com
or by contacting

512 Three Mile Harbor/Hog Creek Rd.
East Hampton, NY 11937
Telephone: 201-957-7185

ISBN 9798492478032

Printed in the United States of America

Dedication

To the loves of my life: Wendy, Cole, and Natalie.
Thanks for being my best teachers.

Table of Contents

Table of Contents

The Power of B2B Social Media

Chapter 1:

Harnessing the Power of B2B Social Media

It's true that the most obvious argument in favor of using social media in business centers on generating consumer awareness, interaction, engagement, reviews, and connectivity. The case for business-to-consumer social marketing is well understood, and most successful consumer products and services companies spend a great deal of time, energy, and resources on these activities—from monitoring their social media platforms and managing their reputations to engaging with followers and promoting awareness. Today, no one needs to write a book on the importance of using social media as part of a business-to-consumer marketing strategy.

But a different story emerges in the areas of B2B companies and nonprofits. When it comes to business-to-business entities and nonprofit organizations,[1] social media is often overlooked and

---

1   I group nonprofits with B2B organizations because many of a nonprofit's stakeholders—which might include corporations, local and state governments, and foundations—are all B2B entities.

undervalued. If an executive realizes its importance, social media may still be de-prioritized in favor of focusing on sales, fundraising, partnership development, and traditional marketing.

> Rare is the B2B enterprise that understands that social media should be a priority—and why.

Regardless, countless marketing executives have told us that social media is *not* a top priority. Other marketing and revenue-generating activities take a front seat to social because no one has taken the time to explain the ancillary value of social media. These executives are not at fault; they just do not have the right information to see the importance of investing time and resources to the effort.

There are organizations that **do** see the value, but they consider social a luxury they cannot afford. Rare is the B2B enterprise or nonprofit that understands that social media should be a priority— and why—and commits the time and energy to deploy a consistent social media program.

And yet, here is something that might shock you: When considering the wide range of objectives a marketing plan might contain, social media can be more effective in advancing a B2B marketing strategy than advancing a B2C marketing agenda. The business-to-business companies that commit to social media marketing use it as a means to an end—not just for social marketing. They view social as an efficacious way of strengthening SEO, disseminating their content marketing messages, and managing their reputations online. In fact, approximately 80 percent of business-to-business marketing specialists who regularly use social media rate it as the single most effective tool of all of their marketing strategies.

Five Common Beliefs of B2B Social Marketing

This book is written for organizations that fall into Beliefs 1 through 4 so they can learn the benefits and value of holding Belief #5.

Belief #1: Social media is mainly for consumer products and services companies.

Belief #2: Social is inconsequential in B2B marketing. There is no reason to pursue this endeavor because ROI cannot be demonstrated.

Belief #3: While our B2B company is putting some resources into social, we aren't seeing the value. It doesn't seem to be moving the needle.

Belief #4: We are not doing all we can to leverage social media. We're not sure how to use it in a more strategic way.

Belief #5:

We see the value of B2B social because we use it in tandem with such marketing activities as online reputation management, thought leadership development, content marketing, and organic search optimization, which are vital to our business.

These five roles of a strategic B2B social media program are:

1. Protecting your reputation online
2. Driving website traffic/strengthening SEO efforts
3. Giving content marketing its power source
4. Increasing your reach through influencers
5. Developing and maintaining thought leadership

The purpose of this book is to share insights on how B2B companies can use social media to impact these areas and attain their marketing, communications, and business goals and objectives. *The Power of B2B Social Media* makes clear several reasons why social is vital in the business-to-business marketing mix and how a B2B "brand" can employ social to protect and promote its reputation.

I wrote *The Power of B2B Social Media* so that I could speak to the many business owners and executives I have not yet met and share with them what we have seen: Using social strategically for B2B marketing can also drive website traffic, help you connect with industry influencers, and assist your organization in enhancing its thought leadership position.

Here is my promise to you: By the time you are halfway through this book, you'll see the benefits of B2B social marketing and understand the key components of a successful program.

I hope you take this experience and harness *The Power of B2B Social Media* to advance your goals. While the rewards may be unexpected, they can be powerful.

— **Chris Rosica**

Chapter 1: Harnessing the Power of B2B Social Media

The Power of B2B Social Media

Chapter 2:

Protect Your Reputation Online

In this book, I demonstrate five compelling reasons to incorporate social media into your B2B marketing plan, but perhaps the biggest and most important reason is this: Social media sites are amongst the most powerful sites in Google's algorithm and hierarchy, putting your company's reputation at risk if you do not proactively manage this critical channel. Social media can be your biggest ally in monitoring and protecting your reputation online, and it can impact several aspects of your business—from recruiting and hiring to generating sales leads.

If you are failing to use social media to intentionally dominate search results for your name, you are leaving too much to chance. In fact, others might be doing it on your behalf, and you might not like what they say. Without giving it much thought, an employee or client could post negative comments about your business on a variety of social channels. A person might write an unfavorable blog or social review, which can be readily found by your key stakeholders, including existing and prospective customers, staff, board members, media, distributors, partners, and other key audiences.

Without social media, you cannot participate in the online conversation. With it, you can monitor perception, contribute, engage, direct, and even redirect the conversation. And, as mentioned, you can use social to populate and control search engine results.

This chapter discusses just five of the ways that social media can help protect your online reputation.

Five Ways Social Media Can Help Protect Your Reputation Online

1. Social media allows you to engage with customers and immediately respond to issues, comments, and crises.

2. Social media sites appear high in search results, and because you can manage most social content, you control the narrative (and your image).

3. Social media allows you to post fresh content in real time, so you can consistently and proactively disseminate positive information about your organization to manage perception.

4. Social media is a tremendous resource for collecting positive reviews about your company, which can markedly influence stakeholder opinion.

5. Social media channels are a great place to disseminate publicity, views, thought leadership, and expertise, which impact reputation and image.

Let us take a look at these one at a time.

1. Social media allows you to engage with customers and immediately respond to issues, comments, and crises.

One Sunday morning, the U.S. Department of Education tweeted a picture of civil rights activist and co-founder of the NAACP, W.E.B. Du Bois, along with a quote: "Education must not simply teach work—it must teach life."

The trouble was: The quote was attributed to W.E.B. DeBois instead of W.E.B. Du Bois.

Twitter took notice with a flurry of roasts. Those who opposed President Trump's then-recent nomination of Betsy DeVos as Secretary of Education were quick to jump in: "Looks like @BetsyDeVos is in charge now!" was followed with, "Betsy DuVos, you mean."

Then came the Department of Education's follow-up: "Post updated - our deepest apologizes for the earlier typo."

> **TIP**
>
> *Never search for your organization's name on Google and then click on a negative article or review. This will only increase the power and visibility of this harmful content. Instead, right click on the link and "open link in new window" or "in incognito window."*

You read that right. The mea culpa tweet contained a typo: *apologizes* instead of *apologies*. It resulted in thousands of comments, an article in *USA Today*, another in *New York Magazine*, and yet another in *Slate*.

Let's remember: This was the Department of Education. While it might be an example of a social media guffaw, it is also an example of the immediacy of social media communication. If you need to disseminate a message, social media is often the fastest, most public way to do so, thereby allowing you to shape the story as it breaks.

Imagine that your company experiences an actual crisis. Perhaps you have to lay off a portion of your workforce, and pundits are making comments about the number of jobs your company has shipped overseas. If you are engaged in the online conversation, you can rapidly disseminate information about the number of new jobs you have created in different divisions here in the United States.

Or, maybe your company experiences an issue of misconduct, an employment practices complaint, or an inflammatory lawsuit. By using social media as part of your marketing strategy, you have a voice and can steer the conversation, direct it, and effectively diffuse or manage the crisis. Without participating in social media, you become the subject of the conversation.

Let's look at a real-life crisis scenario that a hospital client faced involving social media. To maintain our partner's anonymity, we will call this integrated delivery network "Unity Hospital." The company encountered a cyber security breach that compromised sensitive patient information. In addition to smart patient communications, a proactive media relations strategy, planned strategic messaging, and thorough spokesperson preparation and media training, we executed the following on social:

- **Social Monitoring**—We used a variety of free and paid tools, including Google Alerts, TalkWalker, Cision, Keyhole, TweetReach, Hootsuite, Sprout Social, Zoho Social, Brand 24, Buzzlogix, and others. We also removed the Facebook reviews section from the hospital's Facebook page so that people could not leave a disproportionate number of negative reviews.

- **Conflict Resolution Off Social Channels**—When concerned patients posted comments on Facebook, we used Facebook Messenger to send private messages to these people to assure them. By directly connecting with people and taking time to send private messages to them, we created relationships and reduced social media chatter, which helped protect Unity Hospital's reputation. (Note that Instagram, LinkedIn, and Twitter have similar private messaging tools that could be used to connect directly with concerned constituents.)

- **Dissemination of Public Statements & Press Releases**—We utilized social to both manage the message and reassure key stakeholders. We disseminated several quotable statements of facts, which we scripted for the news conference and posted on social.

- **Use of Video**—We created low-production-value videos of the CEO showing concern and talking about the situation and remedies. To show authenticity and to respond immediately, the videos were intentionally simple and not overly produced. They were shared socially and on Unity's website.

These efforts helped to reduce the social media snowball effect. Within a week, the public-facing story fizzled out. The videos offered assurance, concern, and empathy.

In communicating this way, you can manage the initial conversation from the start. Rather than having the media set the tone, you will set the tone, which means you can communicate with sincerity and disclose your plan for containing and addressing problems. When you are proactive in communicating via all marketing channels, including social media, the result is that your company demonstrates it is more than capable of handling the crisis.

If a story such as this breaks, you will want to engage in the conversation regarding the breach—wherever that conversation is happening. Engaging with the people, businesses, and media who are talking about your company makes sound business sense. You cannot stop the conversation, so you might as well do all that you can to make sure the perception of your organization is as positive as possible and that people know your company cares.

All contemporary crisis communications plans include social media protocols, action steps, and communications. However, new social channels are always popping up, so be sure to update your crisis plan annually to ensure all bases are covered and that you are taking advantage of the latest tools and platforms.

Most, if not all, B2B companies—even those that do not commit to a social media strategy with an ongoing thought leadership and content marketing effort—should monitor social. They can respond to negative posts and work to communicate in such a way that builds stakeholder confidence. Keep in mind, though, that this behavior is purely reactive. They might respond to issues and complaints from customers, but the strategy is lacking a proactive approach toward managing an image or reputation.

While this is better than ignoring social commentary altogether, organizations that lack proactive B2B social media plans are overlooking a tremendous opportunity, and they are foregoing the reputation-management benefits that social affords B2B entities.

What happens when there are real stakes and a company is not proactive on social media? Lets look to HSBC, a UK bank with sixteen million business and individual customers. Back in 2015, Apple Pay was launching in the UK, and HSBC was supposed to be one of the banks that allowed Apple Pay. Yet, launch day came, and Apple Pay was not available to HSBC customers.

What did HSBC do? It remained silent.

Rather than letting its customers know in advance that access to Apple Pay would be delayed, HSBC sat back and waited. They did not explain the delay. They did not apologize.

The number of tweets about HSBC skyrocketed, with negative tweets outnumbering positive tweets by a ratio of five to one.

HSBC missed an important opportunity to connect with its customers. Had it announced the delay proactively, customers might have complained, but much less so. Beyond that, HSBC would have been part of the conversation, and not the topic of negative conversation.

HSBC could have said something like, "Like you, we are eager to see Apple Pay available to the businesses and individuals we are proud to call our customers. However, the launch of Apple Pay for HSBC will be delayed as we address a few important aspects of the Apple Pay/HSBC interface. We want our customers to have a positive experience with every transaction, and we believe that by continuing to enhance our interface as it works with Apple Pay, our customers will appreciate the user-friendly platform when we launch our partnership with Apple Pay in approximately two weeks. Thank you for your patience, and please let us know if you have any questions."

> **TIP**
>
> *As much as possible, monitor what people are saying about your company in real time. For instance, you may want to respond publicly to a post on your Facebook wall so other customers see your concern and the solution you are suggesting. Or, if you pull a comment down because it is inappropriate or vulgar, message the individual privately and try to address the situation. Also, you may want to turn off reviews on your FB business page.*

This would not have eliminated all of the disappointment, and while some people would have complained nonetheless, at least HSBC would have been in charge of directing the conversation.

Failing to address the matter raised all sorts of questions in customers' minds as to when and whether Apple Pay would be available through HSBC. Surely, customers eager to have access to Apple Pay wanted to jump ship, worried that they would need to bank elsewhere. HSBC could have averted many of the negative mentions with a few simple social announcements. The company seemed to learn its lesson: When Apple Pay became available a couple of weeks later, it let its customers know in advance.

> **TIP**
>
> *Always be positive and state the facts. Take the high road, even if your company is being attacked. Responding to insults in kind, passing the buck, or pointing fingers only prolongs negativity. Your company will fare better in the long run if you can respond to criticism with concern and dignity.*

Keeping an eye on the online conversation allows you to respond with assertive communications that protect your reputation should any negative information appear in search results. Our online reputation management and search marketing division has built a tool that aggregates information and prepares trend reports. While there are numerous options for monitoring and evaluating online sentiment, the fact is that companies can monitor social and search results (plus news), the two most important components, on their own and take basic preemptive measures without incurring excessive costs.

Here are a few tips for using social media to address any negative publicity and comments online:

1. First, subscribe to Google Alerts, which notifies you anytime your company, product, or people are mentioned online. If you are deluged with comments, you might need a more sophisticated tool. If your company is generally under-the-radar, Google Alerts allows you to monitor the online conversation without too much hassle. We also use Talkwalker (https://www.talkwalker.com/alerts), another tool that offers quality monitoring at no cost. (Refer to the other social media monitoring tools listed on page 5.)

83 percent of people in one survey reported that they do not trust advertising, while 72 percent said that they trust online reviews.

2. Next, search your company name once or twice weekly on Google and Bing (and on the top social channels). You may also want to monitor AllTop, a popular publishing site. Most importantly, look carefully at the first few pages of search engine results.

If you have one or more negative mentions on page one of search results, including those posted on Glassdoor, Google Places, Yelp,

BBB, review sites, or other complaint aggregators, consider hiring a company that specializes in online reputation management (ORM) to help mitigate the issue and prevent lost business opportunities. However, beware of online reputation subscription models, which seem at first glance to be a value because of the affordability. You generally get what you pay for when it comes to ORM. Making a real impact on a reputation requires time, hard work, and energy, which demands a reasonable investment of resources.

This brings us to the second way that social media can protect your online reputation.

> **TIP**
>
> *Keep pages one and two of Google search positive or clean for your company name. Otherwise, your business is likely to be impacted.*

2. Social media sites appear high in search results, and because you can manage most social content, you control the narrative (your image online).

As you will learn in Chapter Two, the first five results on page one of a search are responsible for nearly 70 percent of all clicks.

With this in mind, it is easy to see why complaints, negative reviews, and information about an organization or issue that appear high in search results can seriously impact credibility, reputation, and sales. In fact, through our ongoing review of our clients' analytics, we have found that if a complaint (a negative social review/post) appears in the first five organic listings of a search result, a B2B organization can expect conversion rates to decrease by 30 to 40 percent or more.

In some business sectors, we have seen conversion rates drop 55-60 percent due to negative content that appears high in an organic search.

We often meet with organizations that have spent thousands, even millions, on advertising, but they do not know what to do about the two negative reviews that appear on page one when another company searches for their brand. Yet, some smaller, more nimble companies we work with employ social media marketing and other tools we will discuss to dominate the first page or two of search results, pushing the occasional negative review or mention to a less-likely-viewed page in search results.

How is this done? The main thing to know is that social media channels appear high in search results. Google places a priority on social sites like LinkedIn, Facebook, Twitter, YouTube, Google My Business, Instagram, and the like. As a result, if you have active social media profiles, they will likely appear on page one of a search result for your company or your key executives' names.

In fact, if someone does a search of your organization's name, your social profiles will almost always appear on page one—especially if you update them with fresh content.

> **DEFINITION**
>
> *A conversion rate is the rate at which a potential customer takes a specific action. For instance, if 100 business owners visit your website, and four of them fill out the form opting-in to receive your newsletter, the conversion rate of your opt-in e-newsletter is four percent.*

With this in mind, it is hard to imagine any reason for failing to establish social media accounts for your organization if only to control page-one search results for your company's name. Managing search means managing perception, so work to manage the message and content potential customers and partners see.

Having social media handles is an easy way to do this, but you must develop content regularly for Google to rank them highly.

Imagine how this plays out in a crisis, such as the one described earlier. If your company has social profiles, not only will these appear on page one, but they can also:

1) Offer messaging to redirect any negative experiences for remediation and manage conversations that are happening about your organization;

2) Help you demonstrate compassion, caring, and professionalism; and

3) Be used as a channel to convey important messaging and information, which, again, helps you shine.

A decade ago, businesses learned the hard way about registering domain names. Nissan.com still is not owned by Nissan Motors, and countless other companies have had to fight hard—and pay big bucks—to reserve domain names. Nowadays, every company knows to purchase not only the dotcom equivalent of its name, but also various extensions.

Why not do the same with social networking sites? Not owning your name on these platforms can be hazardous and can be embarrassing. The alternative is that someone registers a social networking site in your name, and then uses it as a channel to disseminate inaccurate or inappropriate content. To this end, make sure that you own all social media handles in your name, including ones you might never use, such as Reddit, Alignable, and Pinterest.

If you do not want to spend your time updating the less important social networking sites with fresh content, at least post a picture and a description of your business naming it the "official" profile or page. This will take minutes, and it will protect your name forever. Otherwise, you might have to fight for the official page later using the channel's bureaucratic, time-draining process–or through legal channels, which will surely take more time and money.

3. Social media allows you to post fresh content in real time, so you can consistently and proactively disseminate positive information about your organization to manage perception.

A decade ago, some companies we worked with were paying hundreds of thousands of dollars to mail marketing information to their potential customers. With social media, you can accomplish the same thing, more often, without spending on printing or postage (though you may need to hire social-savvy staff to execute and spend some dollars on social advertising). This is not to say direct mail is dead, but the power of social is nearly unlimited.

Social allows you to develop and share a steady stream of content, from tips to commentary to subject matter expect advice. In other words, your content can pop up consistently reminding your potential customers that you are the expert and that you offer smart solutions.

As mentioned, if you proactively build a strong social presence, you can enhance the likelihood that your well-managed social content and profiles appear prominently on search engines so you can manage perception—and your organization's image. If you have strong content marketing, social media, reviews management, PR, and SEO initiatives in place, all of which are described later in this book, you can actually push down negative information that can tarnish your reputation, erode sales, and prevent potential employees from applying for your top jobs.

4. Social media is a tremendous resource for collecting positive reviews about your company, which can markedly influence stakeholders.

When companies receive good or even outstanding service, how often do you think they go online, rave about it to their peers, and become advocates and champions?

Not very often. They just go about their business.

If a company receives bad service, on the other hand, they are a lot more likely to complain. Commonly, they try to reach a solution with the company and fail. Now they want retribution.

They jump online and complain on social sites, and they might even take to Yelp or Google My Places—map listings and reviews. Because these sites, particularly Yelp and Google, have lots of traffic, tons of inbound links, and real reviews from real people, they are regarded as authoritative.

One way or another, you can expect that customers who have negative experiences will be more inclined to leave reviews than customers who have positive experiences, therefore communicating an inaccurate view of your true customer satisfaction levels. We have met with companies that have thousands of happy customers and two dozen negative posts and complaints, but only a handful of positive reviews. The true ratio of satisfied to dissatisfied customers was not reflected in the negative reviews that prominently appeared online, and they lost sales opportunities because of a small percentage of unhappy clients. This demonstrates the importance of managing your online reputation—and of B2B social media.

Reviews pack a lot of punch. In fact, 83 percent of people in one survey reported that they do not trust advertising, while 72 percent said that they trust online reviews as much as personal recommendations from real people. Just how trusted are these peer-review sites? According to a Nielsen survey, peer recommendations are the most credible form of advertising, and when it comes to making a purchasing decision, buyers are 92 percent more likely to trust their peers over an advertisement. Point being: You can find yourself playing defense, and losing, if you are not proactively protecting your image through social means.

While these studies are generally directed toward consumer buying attitudes instead of business attitudes, keep in mind that all buying decisions are made by individuals or groups of individuals. People, whether they are acting on behalf of a company or of a household, read and rely on reviews.

So, if you are in a position to ask your customers to review your products, services, or company online, do it. Try every ethical tactic possible to encourage your happy customers to communicate an enthusiastic opinion about your organization, product, or service online.

Requesting reviews is particularly important if any negative comments appear on page one of search, or if you want to prevent negative reviews from occurring high in search results.

You can make this request online after demonstrating quality service and the value you offer. Depending on your offerings and when customers will recognize quality, you can make the ask one week to six months after purchase. Request a review via an automated email written to solicit feedback and social reviews from clients who are completely satisfied. This email can also provide an opportunity to identify issues that require an immediate fix. See Figure 1 for a sample email.

While we are on the subject of testimonials, it bears noting that you can and should request these from satisfied customers, of course asking permission before posting them on your blog, corporate website, social accounts, and inserting them in your proposals. We suggest using their full name and company, wherever possible, and obtaining a waiver to use it. If you work in a highly regulated industry or cannot obtain permission to use their full name, use the customer's first name and last initial, assuming they are amenable. Third-party endorsements are valuable across the board, so do not simply hang thank you letters you receive from customers in the break room. Write back and ask if you can post the letter on your website and share them through social media.

> **TIP**
>
> *Include relevant search terms & key phrases in article and news release headlines so that when media outlets and blogs cover your company, this content will appear higher in search.*

We should also mention that reviews must be authentic. Today's consumers are smarter than ever, and they can spot phony ones a mile away. Genuine reviews from truly happy customers look and sound different than reviews created by a company representative for the purpose of tricking potential customers into buying a product or service. Rest assured, customers will see right through any attempt at deception (Google and Yelp are constantly getting smarter about this, too).

Figure 1: Sample Email[1]

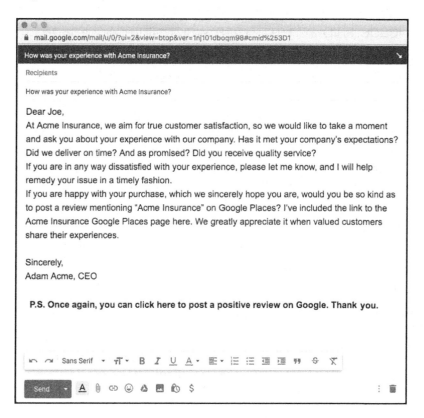

5. Social media channels are a great place to disseminate publicity, commentary, thought leadership, and expertise, which all impact image.

Here is another way social media can help you protect your reputation: Google and other search engines consider media outlets to be authoritative due to their credibility, fresh content, and heavy Web traffic. This means that if you secure earned media coverage, it can rank high in Google's algorithm—particularly if you syndicate synopses of the articles on your blog, a powerful social tool, with links to this content online. Then, use SEO tactics, such as link building on the Web, to promote it. This enables you to leverage positive media mentions of your company to control search results (per the next chapter about driving website traffic).

> **TIP**
>
> *In addition to syndicating and promoting media coverage (third-party endorsements) on social channels and the web, it's always smart to share them via email marketing, at tradeshows, and via your sales force—who can use media placements as selling tools, rich with credibility and authority.*

Industry blogs, newspapers, business and trade industry magazines, podcasts, television programs, and radio shows all produce online content. If one of these interviews includes your company, the links might very well appear high on search results *if you syndicate and promote them.*

Your integrated social media strategy, then, should include:

- Social bookmarking of the story.

- Link-building that drives more traffic to the positive news mention (and bumps it higher in a search result).

- Posting mentions of the media article on industry blogs using unique content and links to the original article.

- Sharing it socially on all relevant platforms including the company blog, website, LinkedIn, Facebook, Twitter, Instagram, Pinterest, YouTube (if a video interview or vlog was secured), and other channels.

Strategies for social bookmarking, link building, and the like will be included in the next chapter.

A quick lesson about inbound links: Google still considers pages that have a lot of inbound links to be more authoritative than those with only a few. Links from relevant and credible third-party websites have more power than links originating from the same domain. Therefore, if you link to a positive media mention of your organization, product, service, or name, from a reputable and relevant website or blog, you will help the story appear higher in search results.

Notes

Notes

The Power of B2B Social Media

Chapter 3:

Drive Website Traffic

Today, the majority of mid- to large-sized business-to-business companies, and even small ones, use organic and paid search engine optimization and marketing (SEO and SEM) to attract customers. If you are failing to incorporate organic social into your marketing efforts, though, the marketing dollars you pay for SEO and SEM traffic are being underutilized. What's more, without integrating organic and paid search engine marketing, organic and paid social media, and content marketing, you are likely missing opportunities to drive a larger volume of qualified website traffic.

Irrespective of industry, the benefits of SEO and SEM are apparent: Your organization can benefit from building its online visibility and driving website traffic to attract potential customers and partners, boost brand recognition, and deepen connectivity. This holds true regardless of what you're marketing, be it:

- Nonprofits or foundations.

- Insurance companies selling to businesses and schools.

- Healthcare companies selling medical devices, pharmaceuticals, or supplies.

- Professional services organizations serving businesses such as law firms accounting consultancies, advertising agencies, engineering, or insurance brokerage companies.

- Manufacturers in the food, hospitality, or spirits industries.

- Construction companies.

- Animal health organizations marketing to veterinarians.

- Tech companies that sell to schools.

- Other B2B product or service categories.

Without integrating organic and paid search engine marketing, organic and paid social media, and content marketing, you are likely missing opportunities to drive a larger volume of qualified website traffic.

If you are not using SEO or SEM marketing to generate qualified leads from the Internet, you are missing opportunities to connect with stakeholders, including referral sources, donors, customers, and those with whom you might not otherwise engage. Having a strong

Web presence also enables you to connect with younger and future generations of buyers who rely on the Internet for research, reviews, and content to enhance their knowledge base.

Regardless of what percentage of your business currently comes from online sources, social media is powerful because, as previously stated, the complex algorithm that determines which sites rank highest on Google and other search engines places social media content at the top of the proverbial food chain. In other words, when a business searches for the SEO terms for which you pay or rank for, pages generated from social media sites are displayed prominently.

Before we go any further, let us take a moment to identify the different types of social media sites that exist. Social media sites include the commonly known channels such as Facebook, YouTube, LinkedIn, Twitter, Snapchat, TikTok, and Instagram, as well as:

1) Review and rating sites, such as Yelp

2) Wikis, such as Wikipedia

3) Social directories

4) Forums

5) Blogs

This last one is interesting. While doing research on products or services, people often land on blogs and consume content—including reviews—without even realizing they are on a blog. We will discuss the power of blogs later in the chapter.

When a person searches online for a product or service solution for their organization, the overwhelming majority of the time, the first page of the search engine result will include one or more social media sites, such as Facebook or LinkedIn profiles, blog posts, or reviews. In fact, we evaluated 100 B2B search terms and found that 94 percent of results included social media sites or posts on page one of organic (Google) search listings.[3] Almost every time, the first-page search result included something akin to Wikipedia, a blog, Yelp (or other social review site), YouTube, Facebook, Twitter, LinkedIn, or other social media property.

Here is a sampling from our research, which was performed from our Fair Lawn, New Jersey office: [4]

Search Terms	Social Results on Page One of Google
Construction companies near me	Yelp, Geniebelt's blog
Bergen County law firms	Google Places, Wikipedia
PBM Company NJ	Ranker, Wikipedia, Google Places
Nonprofits Northern NJ	Facebook, Twitter, Wikipedia
Vision insurance	AllAboutVision (blog)
Engineering company NJ	Google Places, Wikipedia

As you can see from this data, when a company searches online to find a resource, read reviews, or identify potential vendors, social media sites nearly always appear on page-one search results. If you are ignoring social because you think it is irrelevant to B2B marketing, your brand is likely missing opportunities to be found online.

3 The appendix lists 50 of the 100 search terms I evaluated. Notice the range of B2B search phrases tested and the social media search results (ranking on Google's page one) for each. This demonstrates the power of social and its importance in harnessing and capturing website traffic and managing perception online.

4 You may already know that search engines serve up local results. In other words, search results almost always vary based on geography. We did not need to include "NJ," "near me," "Bergen County," or other location qualifiers to generate relevant results from search. After all, location-specific phrases are unnecessary based on the fact that all search is local. That said, our investigation was conducted in our Fair Lawn, New Jersey offices, located in Bergen County just twelve miles from New York City. The county is densely populated and home to approximately one million residents.

According to the search analytics experts at Moz, an average of 71.33 percent of searches result in a page-one organic click. On the first page alone, the first five results account for 67.60 percent of all clicks. On the other hand, page two and three get only 5.59 percent of the clicks. Social media, therefore, is an important factor in heightening online visibility as it appears in search results which generate the most clicks and can help drive prospective buyers to your site.

Turn your attention to a Google Heat Map Index, as shown in Figure 2 on the next page. The Google Heat Map Index is a graphical representation of how much activity a listing receives (that is, how many clicks it gets) as a result of a Google search. When a search engine generates a result, the Google Heat Index represents how many of those suggestions are clicked upon. As shown by Google's Heat Map Index, page one results matter most. Since social sites rank tops in algorithm of results, you can see the importance of this in the context of driving website traffic and heightening visibility online.

This is evidence that appearing on page one of a search-engine result equates not only to getting your brand out there, but also to building search traffic and qualified leads for your organization. If you want your organization's search terms to be clicked upon and you want your audience to find their way to your website, use social to build organic search rankings.

Figure 2: Google Heat Map

Google's Heat Map illustrates the importance of dominating search results and securing as much content as possible on page one.

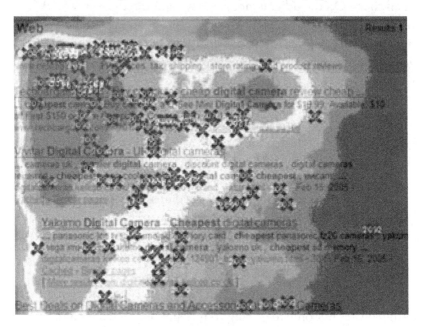

Four Strategies for Using Social Media to Drive Website Traffic in a B2B Business

Herein, we are going to discuss four of the fundamentals of using social media to drive website traffic:

1. Build, update, and optimize your social networking sites.

2. Apply basic SEO strategies to all content disseminated online.

3. Build and syndicate content using a multi-channel approach.

4. Try creating a Wikipedia page.

1. Build, update, and optimize your social networking sites

Social networking sites are just the tip of the iceberg when it comes to social media, but they are important. You may want to consider having individual Facebook and LinkedIn pages, as well as Twitter and Instagram accounts, for your organization, chief executives, and products or services.

These top social networking sites have a ton of traffic and billions of links built to them. Therefore, they have significant "domain authority," meaning Google and other search engines consider them extremely important. It is therefore likely that a Facebook, Instagram, LinkedIn, YouTube, or Twitter profile will appear near the top of a search result, should your company name, product name, or chief executives be searched. As previously discussed, this makes social an important tool in reputation management as well.

> **TIP**
>
> *Keep in mind that when you follow someone on Twitter, they will be more likely to follow you, so keep building the list of important people you follow who work at companies that are critical to your business's success or who have influence in your industry. A percentage will follow you back.*

If you create profiles on these top networking sites, you have gone far to ensure that a few of the page-one search results of your company name will be occupied by the social networking sites you control, which not only can help you dominate for your name but can also manage your image.

Of course, you should then go about updating these sites and profiles with fresh content that places your company, expertise, product, service, or executives in a positive light. A good rule of thumb for B2B companies is to post new content two to three times per week.

You can also:

- Share timely information.
- Connect with your customers.
- Build credibility and influence.
- Grow "share of voice," which is the share of exposure your company receives.
- Track trends and participate in the conversation surrounding them.

You should update your social media sites with content that boosts other page positions in a search result. In short, it works like this: Let's say a news outlet runs a story about your business. If you link to that story from your Facebook, LinkedIn, and Twitter profiles, the story will receive more traffic and can appear higher in a search result. This means you may be pushing yet another positive mention to page one. Through email marketing to your stakeholders (including employees) and other communications, you should encourage them to like and share your social content.

> **TIP**
>
> *Use hashtags in your social posts to gain additional views and get in front of new audiences. The hashtags should be related to the content of your post or the sentiment of the post for the highest chances of engagement with your social content.*

Anthony Church, formerly of Interact Marketing, advises his clients to always link their websites to their official social media channels and then use those social media channels for opportunities to link back to their company website. Schema tags can also be built into a website to help Google understand the official social media accounts related to the website.

"When you do all this, it helps search engines understand that all of this content is interrelated," said Church. "Search algorithms are looking at social signals, so if you are active on social media platforms, search engines will see that and conclude: *Okay, we have identified three social media profiles related to this company and they all seem to be active.* Having an active social media presence, and making sure the websites and social media sites link to each other, can have positive impacts on search engine optimization."

As for optimizing your accounts for engagement, keep in mind that social media optimization is not as technical as search engine optimization, and, unfortunately, the largest social platforms limit the value of organic social content optimization to encourage more advertising on their channels.

> **TIP**
>
> *Be smart about your hashtags. Using hashtags that are already extremely popular and widely used might mean your content is getting lost. On the other hand, using a hashtag that is barely used at all may also mean that it never gets seen. Thus, in addition to the popular hashtags (i.e., #motivationmonday) try to incorporate some that are more moderately used.*

You can optimize your social channels by following a few rules:

- Add images when it is an option.

- Sprinkle your keywords throughout your bio or "about" sections.

- Fully complete the account information so that your profile is as robust as possible.

- Link to your website(s) and blog(s) from your social sites.

- Stay active on social.

- Showcase your brand's voice through clever and conversational copy.

- Supplement organic social efforts with paid social tactics, such as boosted posts and ads.

2. Apply basic SEO strategies to all content disseminated online.

This book is not a tutorial on SEO.

Indeed, we would need to devote an entire volume to cover the basics of today's most efficacious SEO strategies as they relate to social. With this in mind, many of the strategies recommended in this book will be ineffective if you do not optimize your Web content. Optimizing content is vital if you aspire to command the attention of search engines. Later, I will suggest that you write and distribute quality blog content and online news releases, but the truth is: You can build and distribute all the content you want, but no one will see it unless it is written about trending topics and includes quality references, links, and optimized keywords–then effectively promoted online.

Therefore, we will cover a few of the basic definitions and ideas here so that you can get to work applying our recommendations.

Search engine optimization is complex and ever changing. Companies packed with search experts have analyzed Google trends and evaluated the algorithm that determines where pages rank and how. But, if your company needs major online reputation damage control, a do-it-yourself mentality about SEO, online PR, and content development is probably insufficient. But if you want to proactively dominate page one for your name as a preemptive measure, there are a few things you can do without necessarily engaging the professionals.

Counter to what some Web marketers say today, the more links you have to your site, the better your company's site will rank on all search engines.

Before we get to that, let us take a moment to discuss keywords. As you probably know, a keyword or key phrase is a basic search marketing term. To find a company, another business might Google a name (if known to them), or, more commonly, it will search for terms that describe the types of products or services the business is looking for. Terms such as "corporate law firm" and "real estate law practice," for example, are ones that can help businesses locate law firms offering these services in their geographic area.

Here is a brief tutorial on SEO strategies that will help your social Web pages appear higher in search results.

- Include your company name, product, or brand in headlines, and ask anyone posting positive reviews (through your review program) to do the same. Also include your name in conjunction with relevant search terms for which you want to rank. A few mentions within an article or blog is sufficient as you do not want to engage in "keyword cramming."

- Familiarize yourself with social bookmarking sites and

bookmark the content you develop, as well as positive mentions posted by other sources.

- When linking, always use your search terms as the anchor text. For instance, instead of hyperlinking "click here," hyperlink your company's name, or better yet, build a link from a relevant descriptor to your homepage. This allows Google to see the association between your page and a search term.

Social media is powerful because the complex algorithm that determines which sites rank highest on Google and other search engines places social media content at the top of the proverbial food chain.

- Title and tag your website's images and videos with your keywords. Stock photos often have keywords associated with them that describe the photo, but oftentimes these terms are not relevant to a business. Change the keywords of these photos so that they include your business name and any other keywords important to your company, even if they have nothing to do with the image.

- Deliver "link power" to sites you want to promote. If a blogger posts a positive review that you want to appear high in search traffic, be sure to link to the review from your social networking sites, your blog, your company's website, and other industry blogs/sites. This will allow the positive blog to appear higher in search results. You should also encourage stakeholders, including employees, to share and like positive articles, blog posts, and social posts. Likewise, link from your social sites to your website and blog, and vice versa.

- Add schema tags to your website and blog alerting Google of the official social media profiles associated with these pages.

- Two pages from the same domain may appear on page one of a search.[5] This means that your corporate website's homepage, as well as a back page might come up on the first page of a search result—good news for reputation management, driving website traffic, and managing perception online.

> *You can build and distribute all the content you want, but no one will see it unless it is written about trending topics, keyword-rich, search-optimized, and effectively promoted online.*

To leverage this potential, start by promoting your homepage and the other pages on your site that are indexed by Google; this information is free and can be found inside Google Search Console. By properly optimizing the site itself, developing fresh content for social and the site itself, and creating inbound links, the page can appear in one of the top slots. Once you have secured this positioning, begin working on some key back pages, the ones people stay longest and visit most on your site (details for which can be readily found in Google Analytics).

---

5   We have seen as many as four pages from the same domain rank from page one. That said, this is rare and happens only with highly authoritative sites that have tremendous SEO power. In most cases, search engines will never list more than two websites from the same domain.

Make sure the page you choose follows all the rules listed:

- ▸ Include the search term in headlines, titles, image names and tags.

- ▸ Use the search term a few times within the content.

- ▸ Have social bookmarks leading to the page.

- ▸ Link to the page (and ask others to do the same) using the proper anchor text.

- Finally, never engage in unethical or "black hat" tactics. Google's algorithm is smart. We have seen this search powerhouse push a company's own website to page three or four of a search result because the company was trying to be clever and trick the algorithm. As mentioned, Google penalizes for keyword cramming, which is the practice of forcing a search term as many times as possible into an article. Years ago, the search giant caught on when companies buried keywords in the footer using a white font, which website visitors could not see but search engine crawlers could detect. Google also penalizes for selling or exchanging links with irrelevant and suspect sites so as to artificially bump up a company or search term, so avoid link farms.

3. Build and syndicate content using a multi-channel approach

The idea here is this: A multi-faceted approach to building and syndicating content allows you to extend your reach and capture more Web traffic.

First and foremost, reaching out through a variety of channels allows you to integrate your marketing message to reach the largest audience possible. Liken all the social media outlets to a traditional marketing campaign. You might use trade media advertising, email marketing, and conferences or tradeshows, all with the goal of reaching your potential customers wherever they may be.

The same philosophy applies online. Most people who engage with your company through the Internet will do so through search, but the way they search will differ. Some will be drawn to blogs, some interact only on social networking channels, and some will be more interested in a corporate website. Still others will rely heavily on reviews. And, existing or prospective investors may regularly look at news. Therefore, search results will best draw in stakeholders if you provide multiple channels with unique content. Search engines are programmed to ignore "duplicate content," so provide a variety of sources with fresh, updated content. This means you that you should create your own content and that you should summarize or synopsize this content plus positive editorial coverage about your organization, inserting one or two links prior to syndication. By doing this, you can help bump an original source higher in search results.

The other reason for using cross promotion is this: If you take a layered approach to building and syndicating content, you can send your traffic to various social channels. After all, a business that's interested in one piece of information about your business available on your blog will likely be attracted to related content posted on YouTube. You can send more traffic to your social channels if you intentionally use them to cross-promote each other, and you can let Google know that all the content is interrelated, which has a positive impact on SEO.

Before we talk more about this, let's play devil's advocate: *Why bother? If I am able to snag the interest of a potential client through my LinkedIn page, why send them to my blog?*

The answer is two-fold: First, the more deeply connected a

company feels to you, the more likely they are to conduct business with you. Think about it like this: If you watch cntent that you love on YouTube, and that leads you to a piece of free content on the company's website, you are significantly more likely to think: *Wow, this company is an expert in an area that's of interest to me!*

Second, traffic drives traffic. Google favors sites that have higher traffic numbers, so if you have an opportunity to attract more qualified search volume using social, do it.

With this in mind, here are two ways to build and syndicate content:

1. *Submit guest articles to relevant industry blogs and publications. Be sure that your own blog, social networking pages, and corporate website all include links to the guest articles.*

   Let's say, for instance, that your company created the Wonder Widget, and you submit a never-before-published article to *Widget World Weekly*. When the article is published, you would then link to the article posted on *Widget World Weekly* from your Facebook page, your LinkedIn page, your Twitter account, your corporate website, and your blog.

2. *Summarize any press releases, news stories, or blog reviews that were written about your product or company and post these summaries on your own social sites, website, and your blog, linking to the original source.*

   Again, keep in mind that Google and other search engines ignore duplicate content, as well as links generated from duplicate content. If you post the same summary on all of your social media sites, all but one will be ignored. As such, rewrite the summaries for each site and insert two or three keywords you would like to rank for, thereby promoting the original article with as many inbound links and social bookmarks as possible. This may take an extra fifteen minutes of your time, but it is well worth it.

Using the Wonder Widget example, let's say that another blogger in the Widget industry creates a glowing recommendation of your product and posts it on his/her blog, Widget Mania. You can then post a freshly worded summary of the Widget Mania article on your own company blog and—here is the critical part—linking to the Widget Mania recommendation from within your summary.

You'll write another summary, again linking to Widget Mania for your Facebook page; another for your website; and so on.

4. Try creating a Wikipedia page

As we know, Wikipedia constitutes a social media site in that is comprised of user-generated content edited by an open community. It draws heavy traffic and is therefore considered highly authoritative by Google's standards, so this site's listings naturally appear very high in search results.

> **TIP**
>
> *On Wikipedia, be sure to reference content from reputable sources only*

Make sure to review Wikipedia's editorial policies to determine whether your company, brand, product, or executives fit the criteria to have pages on Wikipedia. Avoid referencing your own website or blog when incorporating citations on your entry and do not include any opinion-based or improvable claims. Entries must be objective, so stick to the facts when creating this content.

It is important to cite credible, third-party references and proof points, such as data, news sources, white papers, or studies.

Likewise, edit the Wikipedia listing anytime a reputable news source covers your company, product, or brand. If a trade or business publication writes a story about your company, cite the article to show that your content is objective and uncontestable. One of the factors this social encyclopedia looks at is whether a person or company has been widely published or publicized often, and in credible journals, publications, or industry analyst reports. The earned media coverage our PR firm generates in trade magazines and business publications unmistakably helps our clients create Wikipedia entries that stick. It is amazing how successful this strategy has been for even small and mid-sized companies.

Other best practices include looking at other, successful Wikipedia entries in your industry and modeling yours after them and regularly reviewing moderator comments to ensure the post meets their changing criteria.

Of course, you can link to the entry from your corporate website and blog to drive the Wikipedia listing even higher. Once it appears, the Wikipedia link should appear high in a search results for your name, which will go far to protect your brand and build credibility.

Final Thought

Unlike email campaigns and other forms of direct marketing, a company has multiple opportunities each day to reach its stakeholders. If you have valuable content that your customers or clients want or need, social media post frequency can happen daily, or even more often—but only if engagement levels are high. It demonstrates that you bring value.

So, what kind of things should you be posting? Keep reading: The next chapter reveals the best kind of content to release on your social channels.

Chapter 3: Drive Website Traffic

Notes

Notes

The Power of B2B Social Media

Chapter 4:

Give Content Marketing Its Power Source

Over the years, many buyers and customers have built up a so-called "advertisement immunity" due to the overwhelming number of ads, popups, and banners they have been forced to endure. Think back twenty years ago, when direct mail was still popular and highly effective. We tossed most pieces of direct mail in the trash, though, from time-to-time, clever pieces piqued our interest.

Metaphorically speaking, we are doing the same with online ads. Ads, particularly those on social sites, certainly can be hyper-targeted to reach the right customer at the right time, but many organizations do not effectively use online ads. As a result, consumers ignore all but the most strategically placed ads. Though the right organic and paid social and search marketing efforts will help you convert a percentage of clicks/views into customers, at a cost that makes sense, the truth is that online advertising has become very costly.

(By the way, and this is outside of the scope of this book, I am a proponent of testing direct mail as part of your marketing program. Why? Because it's viewed as an old-school practice and often ignored. I receive approximately 1,000 emails for each piece of direct mail that comes my way. So if you have compelling creative, and a smart, attention-getting campaign, it's worth testing this channel.)

If your online advertising and email marketing become less effective, employ fresh, valuable content in your marketing efforts. Buyers want authenticity and look to thought leaders for tips and advice. They want to know that they are buying something valuable from a reputable source.

The Golden Rule of content marketing is this: the more valuable, data-rich, trending, and memorable the content, the better the results.

This is where content marketing comes into play. Content marketing is the practice of creating and distributing free, valuable content related to your area of expertise (product or service). Content takes many forms. It could be a white paper, a podcast, a video tutorial, an e-book, infographic, or anything else you give to your constituents for free.

Keep in mind, most Americans, particularly younger generations, are much more inclined to watch videos and consume infographics and photos. In fact, it is estimated that by 2025, half of viewers under the age of 32 will not subscribe to a paid TV service in favor of YouTube. In any given month, 80 percent of people ages 18 to

49 watch YouTube, and that YouTube gets more than 30 million visitors each day.

As for copy, most prefer shorter social posts (100 or 200 words) to longer pieces of content. That said, to impact SEO results, longer pieces must also be written for your blog on an ongoing basis as Google's algorithm favor's content that is longer.

An accounting firm that provides tax and bookkeeping services for businesses might, for instance, provide a free white paper advising family-owned businesses how they can transfer the family's intangible capitals—like values—alongside their financial assets. A public relations or digital marketing firm might create a free booklet on best SEO software practices—or write a book such as this. A company that sells CRM software might release free videos about the best practices to build a sales pipeline. A company that sells technology to schools could write a piece about keeping students engaged in a virtual learning environment. *These are all examples of content that can be marketed.*

This is important to know: Content marketing works. Per dollar spent, content marketing gets three times the numbers of leads as paid search. It also generates three times the number of leads than traditional marketing while costing about 62 percent less.

After all, people make buying decisions based on trust. When they believe a company is authentic in their efforts to provide value to their customers and not simply looking to make a sale, they are more likely to purchase from that source. Therefore, due to rising costs and more competition, we are seeing that the best combination includes ad-spends on social and Google's ad network coupled with an emphasis on organic search fueled by PR and content development and marketing.

Ad Spends on Social Channels and
Google's Ad Network

+

Organic Search Fueled by Fresh PR and Content

=

*Strong Formula for B2B or Nonprofit
Brand Awareness*

The truth is, if you are doing any content marketing at all, you would be leaving money on the table if you didn't use social media to disseminate it. Let us take a look at how social can help this process by looking at five strategies for using content in marketing in your B2B social media strategy.

Five Strategies for Using Content Marketing in Your B2B Social Strategy

Here are five reasons to combine content marketing with social:

1. Google's algorithm will pay more attention to your sites if they have new, fresh content.

2. Content marketing allows you to showcase the value of your business's products or intellectual property.

3. Content marketing feeds your blog (which boosts SEO).

4. Content marketing strengthens your email marketing efforts.

5. Video content will promote your YouTube and other video-sharing channels.

1. Google's algorithm will pay more attention to your sites if they have new, fresh content

If you want to elevate your online search ranking/position, Google's algorithm requires you to create quality content that is fresh, unique, and educational—which is one of the many arguments in favor of content marketing. Your white papers, videos, websites, or other content will drive awareness of your brand higher in organic searches.

What better place to release and disseminate these critical marketing pieces than social media? About 92 percent of B2B companies are already creating and marketing content in the form of white papers, booklets, video tutorials, information, podcasts, and the like. If you are engaged in content marketing, you want it to be seen by as many people as possible—and social can help.

After content is written and placed, it can and should be synopsized, optimized (with hashtags and a few essential key words) and syndicated on blogs, socially, in email campaigns, and through social bookmarking. You should also create a cross-linking strategy that allows you to link to the content from as many different places as possible. Why? Because all of these strategies will drive more traffic to the piece, which tells Google the information is important. This, in turn, will increase its ranking, driving even more traffic, while promoting you as an authority.

> ### TIP
> *Your content will be more relevant and secure more engagement if it ties into something happening in the news, or something that is trending on social media sites.*

Failing to use social media to disseminate your content would be like failing to hit "send" on an email. It means lost opportunities. When you regularly update your social sites with new, high-quality content, you remind your potential clients that you offer intelligent, value-based services or products—which creates opportunity. Plus, Google, which loves fresh content, will have a reason to place you higher in search results.

If you want to take it a step further, take advantage of the marketing features that many social sites offer to immediately connect with companies that want to do business with you. Many of these opportunities are paid (advertising). It can pay dividends to boost posts featuring your content, for instance, which can heighten visibility.

Imagine, again, that you own an accounting firm that provides bookkeeping and tax solutions for businesses. As part of your content marketing effort, you might create blogs, videos, and white papers advising on tax-saving strategies, smart bookkeeping strategies, employment and leadership practices that result in the lowest turnover, and a wide range of other topics that can impact a company's bottom line. You can do this—time and time again—by posting on your social sites.

And here's the even better news: 60 percent of people are inspired to look into a product after reading about it.

2. Content marketing allows you to showcase the value of your business's products, services, or intellectual property.

I mentioned earlier that your content could take one of many forms. It could be a white paper, podcast, video, e-book, infographic, or anything else you give to your constituents for free. There is no one-size-fits-all formula for content marketing, but there is one rule.

The Golden Rule of content marketing is this: the more valuable, data-rich, trending, and memorable the content, the better the results.

Often, we meet clients who are afraid to release trade secrets. They worry that if they provide too much information, their potential clients will simply do it themselves. You need not worry about this. The truth is that the more value you offer for free, the higher the perceived value of your paid product or service. Your potential clients will think: *Wow! If this company's free booklet offers this much value, imagine how much value I will get when I hire them or buy their products or services.*

The trade-secret mindset is consistent with the final chapter in my first book, *The Authentic Brand.* The chapter is entitled "Flying

Always ensure unique content across all social platforms.

Under the Radar: A Great Way to Crash and Burn," and makes the case that if you fail to effectively tell your story, someone else will beat you to it. If you want to be noticed, you must have solutions and a valuable story that you thoroughly disseminate to build brand recognition and thought leadership so that you drive sales and dominate your category or region.

Your trade secrets will do you no good if no one knows about your company. Instead of protecting them, use them to prove your company's value.

Ideally, your content will solve a problem you know your audience has (and they realize they have it), and it will be something they will want to share with their colleagues. Posting it on social sends a loud message to the world: *Our brand is in the business of offering, valuable information that you can share with whomever you want.*

In fact, if you can come up with a clever strategy that encourages people to share your content via your social channels, all the better!

> ## TIP
>
> *Use tools like Google's Search Console to inform your content marketing strategy. This tool can help you identify search terms for which your company is appearing in search results. If you are on the bottom of page one, or on page two, you can create content around that search term, increasing the possibility that you will rank higher for a search term you are within "striking distance" of securing.*

3. Blog feeds your content marketing.

Let's say your company sells point of care (POC) advertising. For illustration purposes, we will call your company "POC World." Of course, you have a corporate website, which should have a blog on it.

Likely, the corporate website will appear on page one of a search for "POC World" with little to no effort. Possibly one or two of your social networking sites also appear on page one if you update them with fresh content. Therefore, you might have secured three of the ten page-one spots with moderate effort.

The on-site blog is very important because you can use it to share new content, which Google values greatly.

Another way to dominate search results and proactively protect your online reputation is to create a separate blog that you own, which conveys information about POC World, tangentially, say for a sub-brand or company division that has its own name. This blog is separate from a corporate website with an entirely different domain (though it bears noting that search engines will surely respond more favorably when your name and links to pages on your site are included on the blog in periodic posts). The

> ## TIP
>
> *Use plugin tools like Sociable to automatically syndicate your content, making it easy for others to share, retweet, and socially bookmark.*

sole purpose of this microsite should be to distribute important information about the division or sub-brand's focus via content marketing.

You can then link to articles within the POC World blog from your other sites, driving up the blog's status in search engine results. In other words, you will have one more website that can rank on page one of search, so you can more successfully dominate search.

This advice goes for people, too. If you want to make sure that searches of your own name, or of your executives' names, come up clean, you can create a blog or microsite for the CEO as a separate domain, which protects her or his online reputation and goes far to manage perception, which we discussed in Chapter 1.

Once you create the blog or site, you must then update it regularly with content new. We suggest doing this at least once or twice weekly. Posts don't have to be long—as little as 200-300 words is fine in most cases—but be sure to also share your major content marketing pieces. Nothing attracts the attention of search engines faster than high quality freshly updated content. Search engine scripts are written to digest, classify, and rank pictures, images, brochures, copy, and videos, all of which will increase your company's chance of being noticed by Google and smaller search engines.

The most important thing you can do to quickly move the blog or microsite to page one of a search result is to update the content with worthwhile stories, infographics, or videos that:

- Are in the news or trending.

- Mention the firm's name.

- Contain relevant and optimized keywords and phrases.

- Include photos or videos in copy-rich posts that are in the form of copy.

- Contain provocative headlines and search optimized content.

Remember the SEO chapter: To catch the attention of search engines, include posts that use the firm's full name in the title, the lead sentence of the post, and once or twice thereafter. Don't be obnoxious: No one wants to read an article that is clearly written for marketing or SEO purposes. Do make sure, though, to sprinkle the full name here and there. This will allow the blog to more quickly gain traction and appear on page one of search results.

You can also setup your blog to automatically syndicate to Twitter and Facebook, which can save time, but always ensure unique content across all social platforms. The time it takes to slightly modify posts pays off.

When you add a blog to your social media efforts that is fed with your content, you can often dominate one more page one slot, bringing the grand total of online real estate you control to four or five on page one of search results. Be sure to crosslink to the blog from your other sites.

4. Content marketing strengthens your email marketing efforts.

When discussing content marketing, we cannot forget about email marketing. While it is true that email marketing is losing some ground, it is also true that it is low- or no-cost and can still provide a sound return on investment. If you are creating content, you might as well find a way to disseminate it via email, particularly if you can drive your readers to a social site (such as a blog), which will increase traffic and provide more evidence that your various social sites are trustworthy and reputable. It is important to note that if you have a database of stakeholders or customers who know you and look forward to receiving your content, open rates and ROI will reflect it. Nowadays, intuitive email marketing and marketing automation software makes it relatively easy to execute and measure ROI.

5. Content marketing using videos via YouTube and other video-sharing sites.

YouTube represents another way to distribute content, and it can have the added benefit of helping you capture a top spot in a search result (when videos are displayed in specific searches, depending on the search term). The second largest search engine in the world, most know YouTube is owned by Google, which means Google naturally considers it an authoritative source.

This bit of nepotism, coupled with high traffic and lots of inbound links, means that YouTube videos that are search optimized will appear high in Google results, particularly if they are linked to from other sites and receive a large number of views.

When posting content marketing videos on YouTube, link to them from your blog, your corporate website, and your social media sites. Also include titles, tags, and keywords. If possible, become authorized to post on relevant industry blogs and post "blog comments," which typically permit lnks to be included to your content.

Chapter 4: Give Content Marketing Its Power Source

Notes

Notes

The Power of B2B Social Media

Chapter 5:

Increase Your Reach Through Influencer Marketing

Companies that approach marketing from a strategic vantage understand the importance of influencer marketing. It can help build thought leadership, boost social shares, support SEO, impact conference marketing initiatives, assist with online reputation management, and increase sales through the credibilty it generates. Before we go into influencer marketing in more detail, let us take a look at the term.

Influencers are people who have the power to impact a group of people's purchasing decisions because of their relationship with an audience or their positioning as an expert in a given field. One simple example: Imagine that you sell medical equipment to hospitals, long-term care facilities, GPOs, and physicians' offices. You attend an industry tradeshow. The keynote speaker at that conference is a well-respected influencer. If that person is on stage and mentions a new PPE solution for front-line caregivers he or she saw at your booth, the speaker can influence the attendees—and the industry.

An influencer can also be a blogger, a well-regarded writer for a trade publication, an accomplished consultant, industry analyst, or anyone who is credible and has a significant social following. They can also encompass key opinion leaders, subject matter experts, clinicians (doctor, nurse, veterinarian, PhD, etc.), top-rated speakers, professional associations, conference managers, advocacy groups, authors, and other authorities.

Conduct research to identify "micro-influencers." These influencers may have a smaller following, but they often have more influence over their followers.

Here is what they have in common: They influence via social media, which is another reason to be proactively engaged on social channels. Not only will it help you identify the influencers in your market, being engaged on multiple social media channels can connect you with them. Influencers are dedicated to their followers, and they are not likely to help your company if you aren't engaged, engaging, and authentic. Often, this requires sponsorships for posts and content development services, which can help you boost sales and gain tremendous credentials. We can't stress enough the importance of building relationships with influencers—not just paying for a one-time mention.

With this understanding of the term influencer, let us turn to influencer marketing. Influencer marketing is the idea that if a company "markets" to the third-party influencer, this subject matter expert can speak about and recommend the company's products, services, and expertise to the industry (and her/his followers). Going with the example of a company that sells equipment to construction companies, you might provide an industry blogger with early access to a new, game-changing piece of machinery via an exclusive product demo in the hopes that the influencer will write about and recommend the product.

Today, influencers are what the media were a decade ago. An endorsement from the right influencer validates your product or service, positions you as an authority, and builds trust, communicating that you are a safe resource. Highly credible third-party placements from influencers can go far to build trust and close deals. Plus, their online presence can impact not only your social media results but, in some cases, your organic search rankings as well.

However, not every industry is chock full of influencers. For instance, in the pharmacy benefit management (PBM) space, which markets in large part to insurance brokers, consultants, and health plans, there aren't many recognized influencers. After hours of research on behalf of a PBM client, we only came up with a handful of influencers—and most wanted compensation to engage. Compensation for engagement is not out of the question, but it's really hard to become a consultant's go-to vendor without a significant monetary commitment, which is not an easy pill to swallow. If your industry has a limited number of influencers, seek out and build relationships with micro- influencers (those with small but highly-relevant followings) and work to build credibility and visibility through the earned media and thought leadership tactics outlined herein.

Five Strategies for Using Social Media in Conjunction with Influencer Marketing

How can you effectively connect with influencers to advance your overall marketing program? Here are five ways:

1. Be engaged on influencers' social platforms.

2. Used LinkedIn to connect with influencers.

3. Pique their interest.

4. Connect in advance.

5. Retain influencers on a per diem partnership basis.

1. Be engaged on influencers' social platforms.

Leave comments, build rapport, share what you like about their posts, share and re-tweet their views. If you become a fan of their content, they will be more likely to engage in return, share your content, and advocate for your product or service.

Of course, be thoughtful about how you engage. If you leave the same generic comments as everyone else, you will be less likely to receive a response. Be insightful, ask smart questions, and always be polite and supportive.

2. Use LinkedIn to connect with influencers.

LinkedIn allows you to see whether anyone in your network knows a particular influencer. If you find that you have mutual connections, ask them if they can introduce you. Through LinkedIn, your network is typically willing to help.

Be sure, too, to share valuable content with the influencer via LinkedIn.

3. Pique their interest.

Let them know how they can benefit from the relationship. While some people will want to promote your product or service because it truly is exceptional, be sure to let the influencer know how he or she will benefit from being connected to you and your company. They should readily see the benefits of initiating a relationship with your company.

4. Connect in advance.

If the influencer is speaking at a notable conference, try to connect with that person in advance, offering a sneak peek into differentiators, whether it is technology, products, services, data, skills, subject matter expertise, or your company's mission. Make the case for the influencer to mention you during the speech (which can demonstrate their knowledge of the industry and can take you from obscurity to brand awareness). In many cases, speakers are tapped for multiple industries or sectors and need these industry insights on trends. Help each other, and help your business

5. Retain influencers on a per diem or honorarium basis.

If you have opportunities to help influencers, see if you can retain them. For instance, ask them to speak at your conference, to author or co-author a bylined article, or to provide consultative services to your firm. This can go far to build the relationship and leverage their expertise as it relates to yours.

Notes

Notes

The Power of B2B Social Media

Chapter 6:

Develop Thought Leadership

Thought leaders are the go-to people in their field of expertise. They are the subject matter experts considered to have the most informed opinions. Seth Godin is a thought leader in the field of marketing; Gary Vaynerchuk, Verne Harnish, and Dan Sullivan are thought leaders in the field of entrepreneurship; Marissa Mayer is a thought leader in the field of artificial intelligence (AI).

In today's world, thought leadership is the new public relations. It is becoming as important as PR was in the pre-Internet era. Most B2B companies today use earned media, content marketing, speaking engagements, and social media to build their thought leadership.

The pre-Internet, pre-cable television media landscape consisted of a handful of TV networks, terrestrial radio, daily and weekly newspapers, 75 or so national magazines, and a few primary trade publications in each industry. On the other hand, today's media landscape includes a head-spinning array of outlets encompassing satellite radio, thousands of broadcast and cable stations (each offering numerous programs), hundreds of national magazines (with just as many regional ones), countless podcasts, thousands of trade publications and tens of thousands of online business and industry channels—plus an incalculable number of blogger and social sites.

With "media dilution" being a gross understatement, the PR landscape has completely changed. As a result, the perception is that PR's impact has become watered down, creating a vortex that leaves public relations pros looking for ways to demonstrate ROI, add value and meet the demands of smart in-house marketers who require measurement against pre-determined KPIs.

So, how can companies overcome these changes brought about by technology?

Thought leadership is the new public relations.

The answer is clear: thought leadership. It addresses all of the issues that PR faces and, it logically integrates with other marketing disciplines, often leading to increased market share and category domination.

Before exploring how to execute a standout thought leadership program, it's important to define it a little more. Thought leadership is not about being known, but about being known for something. Bill Nye the Science Guy isn't just known: He is known for being the science guy. Mark Zuckerberg is known for being an innovator in social media.

Thought leadership is not just about brand awareness, but the space you occupy in your customers' minds. If you say the name Weili Dai in a tech setting, everyone will know that you are talking about someone famous for her work in semiconductor technology. A thought leader, much like an influencer, is an individual, brand, or company that is recognized as an authority in its field, one with specialized expertise— a trusted and highly sought-after resource with credible, trustworthy subject matter experts or key opinion leaders.

When a company works toward building thought leadership, it can authentically connect with its customer base and dramatically increase demand for its products or services. If it succeeds with this expert positioning, it can even become an industry frontrunner, heightening awareness and brand equity.

Two common questions we're asked include: "How do you develop a thought leadership platform?" And, "How long does it generally take?" Let me answer the latter first: It all depends. The amount of time it takes for you to become a thought leader hinges on the competitive landscape, size of the space you are trying to "own," your budget, internal and external communications staff and bandwidth, the quality and quantity of key opinion leaders or subject matter experts you have on staff or partner with, and many other factors.

Seven Strategies for Using Social Media to Grow Thought Leadership

As for the first question, following are seven essential practices you can deploy to grow thought leadership, brand presence, and market share:

1. Refine your positioning and messaging.
2. Generate earned media.

3. Leverage social media to manage perception.

4. Strengthen your content marketing efforts on social channels.

5. Remember that people create thought leadership.

6. Repurpose and leverage earned media content on social (and elsewhere).

7. Connect with influencers on social channels.

1. Refine your positioning and messaging.

In other words, unearth and articulate your primary differentiators, or as my friend, author Simon Sinek, says, "Know your why." Being known for something that not all your competitors are already focused on should be the foundation on which your positioning and organizational and marketing objectives and activities are built.

After an authentic, meaningful, and compelling positioning statement is established, it is vital to develop audience-specific messages and support them with proof points and real reasons to believe. Real stories, including human-interest and key-opinion-leader-driven narratives, only add credibility and get you noticed. These are brought to life and disseminated through integrated internal and external marketing communications programs—and, no surprise here, your social channels.

Additionally, it is imperative that real life talking points be shared with all sales, marketing, customer service, and other key staff so everyone is telling the same story—a memorable one that resonates with stakeholders. Rule of thumb: Make it relevant, ensure that it resonates, don't mimic what other companies are communicating, and, clearly convey your reasons to believe (proof points), so your business commands attention, respect, and credibility.

2. Generate earned media.

Earned media is the non-paid media coverage you receive through pitching stories to targeted reporters and media outlets. Reporters, bloggers, producers and other media are influencers, so if you want to become a thought leader, find a way to publish byline articles, contribute a Q & A or expert column, conduct television and radio interviews, write or contribute to blogger reviews, or otherwise use media to develop your expert strategy.

These channels also can go far to secure speaking engagements, influence the right people on social media channels, create a compelling story for your customers, and support sales. Since media outlets typically have large social followings, you gain the ability to reach a large audience of stakeholders across multiple social channels including YouTube, Instagram, Twitter, and Facebook. Encourage employees, vendors, customers, partners, and business affiliates to read and share socially these opinion pieces and other earned media content.

3. Leverage social media to manage perception.

We have discussed social media's role in thought leadership. On these platforms, you can share articles, viewpoints, industry news, stories, trends, and information that center on your positioning and your strategic objectives. Here are some additional takeaways:

- Depending on the nature of your business, you can build followings to promote word-of-mouth, influencer advocacy, customer loyalty/recognition, and sales.

- You can use social media to get noticed and secure meetings at conferences and tradeshows.

- With marketing automation tools, you can measure the impact of those interactions, as well as the efficacy of socially integrated email marketing campaigns.

Remember, as an entertainment-based society, it is vital to use video and photos and their corresponding social platforms to tell stories and connect with important audiences. This is a must today and into the foreseeable future.

4. Strengthen your content marketing efforts.

Your content marketing can position you as a thought leader. While content is created when you generate earned media or public relations, it is important to create additional high-quality content, conveying thought leadership in white papers, tips, trend articles, infographics, and videos developed within your content marketing plan.

The video content you create does not (always) need to be too polished. It should look and feel authentic or organic rather than overly produced. In addition, written content also does not need to be tremendously long (though it bears noting that in some industries if you want your content to rank high in search engine results, it will be necessary to develop lengthier articles and content for blog posts due to Google's algorithm).

You can also use your organization's blog as the hub or focal point of your content marketing efforts. This means taking a blog article on a relevant or topical theme and creating unique, synopsized versions for social posts and email campaigns.

Disseminating these attention-getting assets should be systematic. Reaching industry influencers or consumers, whether current customers, media, analysts, circuit speakers, associations, or other stakeholders, should be planned regularly, but not to the point of overkill. As a rule of thumb, we suggest sending such pieces in three- to four-week intervals. You don't want to inundate your contact list, but don't want to be forgotten either.

Customizing content for tradeshows, social, and email is a must. Measuring the impact of your content program can be accomplished through marketing automation software reports, surveys/polls (viewing improvements over time beginning with a baseline brand recognition index), and by monitoring search volume and trends, as well as growth of social connectivity.

5. Remember that people create thought leadership.

Without people, there is no thought leadership. Without people, there is no social media. People not only serve as the conduit by which you secure earned media coverage (media covers people and their views), but their expertise promotes trust and credibility. Key opinion leaders (KOLs) and subject matter experts (SMEs) should be developed from within organizations, while in some industries, such as healthcare, it is wise to tap third-party experts as they offer enhanced credibility. These outside experts can add tremendous value, particularly if they are respected, accredited, and mediagenic.

KOLs should regularly develop articles, white papers, blog posts, and other content and be pitched to speak at conferences, tradeshows, roundtable discussions, podcasts, and webinars. In a B2B environment (such as a new product launch in the healthcare space), these KOLs can be tapped to conduct interviews and satellite media tours, regular columns, podcast interviews, and conference speaking engagements. We typically introduce them to trade and business media for scheduled and future articles and segments.

While people have their individual LinkedIn profiles and Facebook pages, company profiles are vital in the social thought leadership and branding process. Leverage your network and that of your staff and partners to tell the story and position your organization as experts through social!

6. Repurpose and leverage earned media content on social.

Because of media dilution and the population's dwindling attention span, these thought leadership pieces should be leveraged and repurposed across all your communications channels. Publicize them on your blog. Share them on all your social sites and send them via email to your database. We always recommend taking longer articles and synopsizing, search optimizing, and syndicating these.

We urge our clients to leverage media coverage to demonstrate thought leadership. This strategy truly works for the companies, nonprofits, and schools we represent. Earned and original content can and should be syndicated and promoted. This can bolster SEO, social media, direct marketing, online reputation management, and conference marketing communications. When a media placement runs or airs, it should be properly syndicated through social channels including your blog, and in email marketing and direct mail campaigns. Again, prior to sharing this highly credible/trustworthy content, it should be summarized, and search optimized through the insertion of key words and phrases your customers or stakeholders are searching for online.

As previously stated, it is also important to name videos and photos using these keywords/phrases, as well as use alt tags to promote these online. Direct marketing of this repurposed content can help you influence stakeholder perception, secure appointments and generate buzz at tradeshows, promote events, schedule appointments and meetings, book showroom visits, and prompt referrals. Third-party endorsements from media and other influencers unquestionably influence the sales cycle.

With the help of modest SEO efforts, you can promote media placements and other content to manage perception and visibility online. This not only heightens thought leadership, but it can also help manage your image.

7. Connect with influencers on social channels.

Know who they are, follow them, like and share their posts, and comment on articles you genuinely like or value. The point here is to engage with them so they are more likely to follow you back and engage with you. All of these things can help you get their attention and begin the relationship-building process, which will bring more awareness to your organization.

A positive online reputation and increasing share of voice online are the byproducts of all seven activities working in tandem, with the aid of an ethical SEO program to promote a company's news, views, social content, expertise and other thought leadership content.

Notes

Notes

Chapter 7:

The Index of Social Media Strategies

This chapter is an index summarizing the best practices that our PR and digital marketing teams have discovered over the years. Some of these insights came from my interview with Anthony Church of Interact Marketing. The following includes specific social channels and B2B practices as they apply to the various strategies and social channels. Keep in mind that this is a brief overview and is not intended to be an exhaustive explanation of each social channel or strategy. My hope is that it is enough of an overview to direct your own research in order to gain even deeper insights.

Social Channels

Facebook

Some social media sites, like TikTok and Snapchat, tend to have a much younger user base while Facebook's average user-age has increased significantly since it launched (now just over 40 years old), though it still has a user base with a large age range. In June of 2021 Pew Reserch reported that 77 percent of women and 61 percent of men use this platform.

Facebook is one of the best social media channels for driving website referrals so keeping it updated is important.

Here is what you should know about the best practices for your Facebook account:

- The account should be following all relevant media, editors, celebrities, experts, thought leaders, etc. that are related to your industry/market. The more accounts you follow, the more likely it is that those accounts (and more) will follow you back, thus giving you an opportunity to build a relationship with them.

- Complete your entire Facebook profile, and sprinkle in some of the keywords you want to dominate.

As for sharing content:

- Keep your posts relatively concise if possible.

  ▶ That said, Facebook is a great platform to share more in-depth information when appropriate or warranted, as there is virtually no character limit. Posts should always include a visual aspect, as photo and video content work particularly well on Facebook and allow others to share in a visually appealing way.

- Links are the best posts for engagements. Images and video are also good. Try to avoid posts that are text-only.

- Try to differentiate content from your other platforms, but your account could have Twitter and Instagram content automatically shared on your feed so there is always activity to keep the account robust.

- Use Facebook Stories, a visual way to share content.

- Don't make your posts sound like ads. Facebook will limit the post's reach if it sounds like an unpaid ad.

- Share relevant articles and current events that relate to your business and that your audience would find valuable.

- Share media placements and tag the outlet and editor, if appropriate.

- Though best times to post change over time (e.g., during COVID-19), the best posting times are typically Sundays, Thursdays, Fridays, and Saturday, with 1 p.m. posts getting the most shares and 3 p.m. posts getting the most clicks.

- Share behind-the-scenes posts as they give your social media followers a sense of being "in the know" before others and help them connect with you at a deeper level.

  ► Livestreaming on Facebook with Facebook Live is a tool that brands can use to keep followers in the loop during events.

- Hashtags aren't as frequently used on Facebook, nor should they be. One hashtag per post will suffice—or avoid them entirely. While you are able to search via hashtags on Facebook, the practice isn't common.

- Cross-reference your other social sites, particularly if you are posting different content. For instance, you might be live-tweeting about a conference you are attending virtually or in-person. Be sure to let your Facebook followers know by posting something like, "Follow us on Twitter for live updates."

- Experiment with stories as they are becoming a more and more popular way of reaching an audience.

In terms of connecting with other people:

- To raise Facebook engagement, frequently "like" and comment on posts from people in your industry, particularly thought leaders and the media.

- Search for Facebook users who have talked about your product/industry and reach out to them offering product/service in exchange for a Facebook post or sponsored content.

- Pay for sponsored posts on Facebook accounts. Sponsored posts can range anywhere from a few dollars to several hundred or even thousands. When searching for a sponsor, target Facebook users/bloggers with a higher number of likes or a very engaged audience.

Speaking of advertising:

- Boost Facebook posts to reach a wider audience.

- Place ads in targeted ZIP codes based on affinity or interest categories.

Instagram

Instagram has more than 1 billion active monthly users as of January 2021, more than two thirds of Instagram users were 34 years of age or younger. This channel is ideal for reaching a new generation of customers, donors, or stakeholders.

That said, Instagram, along with Snapchat, are great places for targeting Generation Z, so if your business is doing business with companies headed by a Gen Z, have an Instagram account for your brand.

Here are some best practices for Instagram:

- As with Facebook, be sure all of your account information is complete. Since Instagram does not allow clickable links within captions, include your website or a promotional URL in your bio. Update this clickable link anytime you are promoting something. Be sure, too, to sprinkle some of your keywords into your bio.

- Follow all relevant media, editors, celebrities, experts, thought leaders, etc. that are related to your industry/market. The more accounts you follow, the more likely it is that those accounts (and more) will follow you back.

- Use Instagram Stories regularly to infuse photos and videos into the narrative.

As for sharing content:

- Post Instagram Stories at least three times a week.
  - ► This keeps your followers up-to-date on company news between posts.

- Post Instagram photos to your feed *at least* three times a week.

- ▸ Include lifestyle photography.

- ▸ Create organic content that is not over-produced or staged.

- Videos get the highest levels of engagement and should be posted as often as possible.

- Make sure videos are easily understood even without sound; *85% of video clips are watched in silence.

- Content should:

  - ▸ Provide value to your audience.

  - ▸ Share behind-the-scenes information.

  - ▸ Be interesting to your audience.

  - ▸ Promote upcoming news and events.

  - ▸ Feature specials and coupons with branded graphics.

  - ▸ Highlight new products and events.

- That said, be sure to have a healthy mix of promotional pieces and non-promotional pieces. If your account is all promotional, people will unfollow you.

- Remember to differentiate your Instagram content from your other platforms, but your account could have Twitter and Facebook content automatically shared on your feed so there is always activity to keep the account robust.

- Always tag influencers (ask for permission if you think the photo might be controversial or unflattering) in your posts.

- Here are the best times for posting on Instagram:

▶ Instagram prioritizes new content, so you should post when people are most likely to be active on Instagram, which, on average, tends to be between 10 a.m. and 3 p.m. CDT. [Ibid.] However, data changes a little based on days, so here are a few other times to consider posting (all times are CDT):

> Post from 8 a.m–2 p.m. on Sundays (this is a low engagement day).

> Post from 11 a.m.–2 p.m. on Mondays.

> Post from 10 a.m.–3 p.m. on Tuesdays.

> Post from 7 a.m.–4 p.m. on Wednesdays (engagement peaks between 11 a.m.–2 p.m.).

> Post from 10 a.m.–2 p.m., and from 6 p.m.–7p.m. on Thursdays.

> Post from 9 a.m.–2 p.m. on Fridays.

> Post from 9 a.m–11 a.m. on Saturdays (this is generally a low engagement day).

▶ That said, statistics on the best times to post change all of the time in conjunction with a change in people's social habits, and your specific constituents may have different behavior. They also vary drastically by industry. So, test these times, find out what works best for you, and post then! Note, different sources publish varying opinions on optimal times to post, making it even more important to conduct testing. You can get first-hand data from the Insights section on the Instagram app. Take a look there to understand when most people are engaging with your content, where they tend to be located, and for other great insights.

Instagram, like other sites, is constantly updating its app to add new features. Be sure to check out:

- The swipe-up feature, which directs followers to websites (only available after reaching 10,000 followers).

- Location, hashtag, and other sticker features for stories, such as:

  ▸ The "ask me a question" sticker, which helps to engage with followers.

  ▸ The music sticker to share your current playlist.

> **TIP**
>
> *When posting videos on social media sites, be sure to add subtitles as many viewers will watch the videos without sound, and most social media sites mute the videos as a default setting.*

- Video apps such as Boomerang, which captures GIF like videos, or the Lapse It app, which creates time-lapse videos.

- IGTV for long-form video content and editorial-style videos.

- Video chat in direct messages.

When growing your Instagram brand, be sure to target influential Instagram users asking for a sponsored post highlighting your product/company, using branded hashtags, and tagging your account in the post. Start by reaching out to ten or fifteen accounts. Based on your response, increase your outreach as needed.

When you are at tradeshows or other events:

- Share photos of the booth/event space from before, during, and after the event.

- Use hashtags that are relevant to your company and the specific event (most tradeshows have a branded hashtag).

- Tag partners and customers in the photos (with consent) and thank them for their attendance.

- Geotag your location.

  ▶ Only about five percent of Instagram posts have geo-tags, but those that do have almost 80 percent more engagement.

Unlike Facebook, Instagram relies heavily on hashtags, which are a great way to amplify reach and search capabilities. Users can search by hashtags to see photos that they are interested in based off their personal interests and likes. By using hashtags in a post, your photo has more opportunity to be seen by your target audience and therefore generate more likes and interaction.

What is the right number of hashtags? Opinions vary, but if you place hashtags at the end of your post, you can get away with using a couple dozen. Be sure that they are related to your post, though! Just like you wouldn't want to stuff a bunch of keywords into an article, you don't want to cram hashtags into the post unless they truly are relevant to the post.

LinkedIn

LinkedIn is used primarily by individuals in a professional capacity, so your business's key executives should have a strong LinkedIn presence as it will help them make new connections and build their brand.

Unlike other social media sites, which have varied practices in terms of outreach, those on LinkedIn are expected to expand their network by doing outreach to professionals they might not know. In other words, have a strong plan for connecting with influencers, potential customers, strategically aligned individuals, and media.

Then, be active by sharing unique and repurposed content relevant to your industry.

- Post shared content two to five times a week.

  ► Repost relevant articles from your industry and create a conversation by asking a question or sharing your point of view on the topic

- Post original content at least twice a week.

  ► Repurpose media placements with a quick synopsis and link to the original article.

  ► Share company/spokesperson bylines.

  ► Post job listings.

  ► Share company or client blog posts to build thought leadership.

- According to Hubspot (July, 2021), the best time to post LinkedIn content varies by industry as well. For example, healthcare and higher-ed organizations should post from 11 a.m. to 1 p.m. (in your time zone). While statistics on the best times to post change all of the time, test these times, find out what works best, and post then!

As is true for all social media sites, be sure that your "About" section is complete, and update it regularly.

LinkedIn is beginning to more effectively integrate hashtags into its posts, so feel free to add a couple of relevant hashtags.

Keep in mind, too, that you can run paid ads on LinkedIn targeting people in ways that are unavailable elsewhere. You can target your LinkedIn ads to people based on job titles, companies for which they work, and employment or career-related criteria that indicate they fall into a certain market, among other unique targeting capabilities available on their ad platform. LinkedIn ads can be costly so be sure to test campaigns with smaller budgets before commiting to more ad spend.

Also, LinkedIn Company Pages have gained in popularity, so be sure to take advantage of those; update this profile at least once a week.

Twitter

Twitter is considered a news source, so incorporating it into your social media plan is important. Your Twitter account should:

- Be complete.

- Follow all relevant media, editors, celebrities, experts, KOLs, thought leaders, influencers, etc. that are related to your industry/market. The more accounts you follow, the more likely it is that those accounts (and more) will follow you back.

As for content:

- Post at least three tweets a week, which might include original content, a retweet, or a reply.

  ► Retweet posts that interest you, either with your own comment, or just the original tweet.

  ► If you are tagged in a tweet by someone (customer, media, thought leader, influencer, etc.) making a comment or asking about your brand, simply reply to the tweet, remembering that your reply will be public. This also applies if someone in the industry is talking about a topic that relates to your business or industry as a whole.

    > That said, differentiate between trolls and customers making real complaints. Customers making real complaints have a reason rooted in logic. Respond to them! Trolls are complaining just to complain or stoke the fire. Ignore them.

- Between tweets, share syndicated content that entices followers to visit other sites.

- Though you should differentiate your content, you can link your Facebook account to Twitter. This not only provides a flow of content between channels, it also prompts Facebook and Instagram followers to check you out on Twitter.

- Use images and video in your posts as they will typically receive approximately 150 percent more engagement than text-only posts.

- Tag influencers and accounts you work with as it gives them and you more exposure, particularly if they retweet your post.

- The best time to post on Twitter is generally from 9 a.m.–3 p.m. on Wednesdays or Tuesdays betwen 9 a.m.–11a.m.. As with all social channels, B2B posts will get higher engagement during business hours. That said, statistics on the best times to post change all of the time in conjunction with industry and changes in people's social habits, and your specific constituents might have different behavior, so test these times, find out what works best for you, and post then! Forego posting on Saturday or Sunday as weekends see less traffic. Also, when posting on Fridays, try 9 a.m. or 11 a.m..

One of the most important tactics for tradeshows and events is to live tweet throughout the event, providing real-time updates so that followers feel that they are experiencing the event with you. Here are some examples:

- "Our booth is ready and the show floor is about to open!"

- "A picture of our VP of Sales speaking with [insert thought leader's name] at our booth."

- "The show was a success! Thank you to everyone that visited our booth today."

Include photos within the tweets, which might include pictures and videos of the booth/event space from before, during and after the event. As well, use hashtags that are relevant to your company and the specific event (most tradeshows have a branded hashtag).

Speaking of hashtags:

- Because users can search by hashtags, adding them is important as it helps increase your reach.

- Due to the character limit (280 characters) on Twitter, it is difficult to add multiple hashtags. One or two will suffice.

- Make sure you know what a trending hashtag means before using it. A few years back, the frozen pizza company DiGiorno, learned this lesson the hard way. In the midst of a viral hashtag about domestic abuse—#WhyIStayed—DiGiorno posted a tweet that read: "#WhyIStayed You Had Pizza." Intentionally or otherwise, DiGiorno's tweet seemed to be making light of the discussion women were having about why they stayed in abusive relationships. When DiGiorno issued its apology, it stated that it did not know what the hashtag meant before posting the tweet.

  ▸ The moral is: When in doubt, don't Tweet

YouTube

In 2020, 82 percent of Internet traffic was video traffic. In addition, 87 percent of B2B marketing pros report positive ROI from their video content (versus 33 percent in 2015). When it comes to sales, 84 percent say video has helped them generate leads. In years past, the idea of making videos might have felt cumbersome. Find a set. Hire professionals. Make sure the quality is good.

Today, high-quality, overproduced videos feel commercial. Though there is certainly a time and place for creating such videos, most of your videos can be shot with equipment you already have. They can be casual tutorials, snippets from conferences, or interviews you film using your newer model iPhone.

Point being: Produce videos—lots of them—and post them on your firm's own YouTube channel. (A channel is the same as a page or a profile. YouTube uses the term channel to replicate the terminology used with televisions, but don't be confused by the lingo. Creating a YouTube channel is essentially the same idea as creating a Facebook page).

Then: optimize your YouTube channel and your videos:

- Include keywords in the channel profile description.

- Keep your YouTube channel active by posting comments on other channels and adding videos on a weekly basis.

- Place keywords in your video title, description, category, and tags.

B2B Practices

Audience building

Unfortunately, the best way to build your audience is through paid advertising on social media sites. In fact, social media channels even offer specific ad and campaign types geared toward promoting your page and encouraging people to like and follow.

Building a large following organically can take longer, requires a lot of production time. Unless you are lucky enough to be one of the very few who nail it with a positive viral piece of content, expect to go the distance with this strategy.

Content strategy

Your content strategy should consider:

- News and trends that might be relevant to your business that you can tie into your content. This will help you engage with more people.

- Search terms you wish to dominate (rank atop search results).

- Search terms you already dominate or are within striking distance of dominating.

- The most valuable information you can provide to your audience.

- Whether you can collaborate with other influencers/thought leaders in providing content that both your audiences might want.

Database marketing

If you are engaging in database marketing, be sure that social media is integrated into your campaign. Most often, your direct marketing will integrate a CRM program onto your website so that you can run an effective multi-channel campaign attributing traffic and site behavior to various digital marketing channels, including social media.

Once you have used your CRM program to build your database of email addresses and phone numbers, you can use the database creatively to reach people via social media using "customer audiences" and ads on social platforms targeted directly to people who have those email addresses or phone numbers associated with their accounts.

Paid social targeting and retargeting

One of the fastest growing segments of digital marketing revolves around paid social media ads. Because social media sites have changed the algorithms such that you are unable to reach as many of your followers organically as you once could, paid social targeting and retargeting is becoming more and more popular.

Beyond that, by paying for social media ads, you are able to reach audiences beyond your followers. Today, you can reach a target audience based on interests, affinity categories, geography, online behavior, demographics, and via many other forms of targeting.

Because we encourage a multi-channel approach to marketing, consider using paid social ads as part of your campaign. This is the fastest way to grow your reach, and it allows you to boost your content marketing to a group of people who might otherwise never see it.

Recommended social media tools

Social media tools are constantly changing and emerging, so the minute this book goes to print, these tools might be outdated, or there may be new players in the market. Still, it bears looking into:

- SproutSocial, SocialClout, and ShortStack for reaching your audience and engaging with your community.

- Hootsuite and Buffer for scheduling your social media content.

- Google Search Console, which allows you to:

  - ► Identify search terms that result in your company's name, website, social site, product, or service.

Miscellaneous notes

- With respect to social media posts:

  - ► Always make sure your spelling is correct.

  - ► If a hashtag is not integrated into a post, place it at the end with no punctuation following it.

  - ► Engage with people in a conversational tone. Don't sound robotic. Have a voice!

  - ► Use language your audience uses.

Chapter 7: The Index of Social Media Strategies

The Power of B2B Social Media

Appendix

Social Media Results of Our B2B Search Terms

To demonstrate The power of B2B Social Media, here are 100 search phrases and resulting social media pages that appear on page one of organic search results. Please note that organic search results constantly change as Google's algorithm is fluid, ever changing.

1. Advertising Agency
   Clutch (reviews/directory), Google Places, Wikipedia

2. Business Coach
   Hubspot (blog), Google Places, Inc. (blog), BrianTracy (blog)

3. Commercial Bakery
   YouTube, Google Places

4. Commercial Banks for Small Business
   Fundera (blog), Nerd Wallet (blog), Lendgenius (blog)

5. Companies to Partner with Nonprofits
   Causevox (blog)

6. Commercial Architects
   Google Places

7. Commercial Maintenance
   LinkedIn, Google Places

8. Construction Companies
   Yelp, Geniebelt's (blog)

9. Continuing Ed for Insurance
   (no social results on page)

10. Continuing Ed for Realtors
    Google Places

11. Corporate Videos
    RocketStock (blog), Wikipedia, Veed (blog), Spectrecom (blog)

12. Credit Unions for Businesses
    Fundera Blog, Nerd Wallet Blog, Google Places

13. Cyber Security Software
    Wikipedia

14. Dental Supplies
    Glassdoor, Google Places

15. Direct Marketing Company

Clutch, Wikipedia, Google Places

16. Durable Medical Equipment
Wikipedia, Google Places

17. Engineering Company
Google Places, Wikipedia

18. Engineering Firms
Wikipedia, Google Places

19. Facility Maintenance Companies
AmericanRegistry (directory), Google Places

20. Food Distributors
Handshake (directory), Google Places, Wikipedia

21. Food Manufacturing Company
Google Places, Wikipedia, Ranker

22. Food Trade Associations
Wikipedia

23. Garden Hose Manufacture
DirectIndustry (directory/reviews), Google Places

24. Glucose Monitors for Hospitals
.gov, .edu and industry journal articles only (no social results on page)

25. Heavy Construction Company
Wikipedia, Ranker, Google Places, Manta (directory), Forbes (blog)

26. Infection Prevention Solutions
ICT (blog)

27. Internet Security Software
Top10reviews (review site)

28. Law firms
Google Places, Wikipedia

29. Medical Device Companies
Proclinical (blog), Greenlight (blog), Google Places

30. Nonprofit Consultants
Linkedin, Google Places

31. Nonprofits
Facebook, Twitter and Wikipedia

32. Online Marketing Firm
TopSeos (directory), Clutch

33. Paving companies
Google Places

34. PBM Company
Ranker, Wikipedia, Google Places

35. PBM Healthcare
Wikipedia, Modern Healthcare (blog), TheBalanceSMB (blog)

36. Pet Product Manufacturers
Google Places

37. Photocopier machine
Wearetop10 (blog), Google Places, Wikipedia

38. PR Firm
Google Places, Clutch

39. Property-Casualty Insurance
Google Places

40. Resources for Foundations
several .org search results (no social results on page)

41. Self-insured Health Benefits
PeopleKeep (blog), Wikipedia

42. Social Media Agency
Forbes (blog), Clutch

43. Succession Planning for CEO
Forbes (blog)

44. Surgical Supply Companies
MedicalEquipmentAndSuppliesReviews (directory), Google Places

45. Transportation Company
Forbes (blog), Google Places, Wikipedia, HackerNoon (blog)

46. Trucking Company
Google Places

47. Truck Parts
Google Places

48. Veterinary Supplies
    Google Places

49. Vision insurance
    AllAboutVision (blog)

50. Pet Marketing Companies
    WorkingWithDog (blog), Marketplace (Blog), Google places

Bibliography

A Guide to Marketing Genius: Content Marketing. Retrieved from https://www.demandmetric.com/content/content-marketing-infographic

Ackerman, T. (2018, July 26). How B2B and B2C Marketing Are Converging Today. Forbes. Retrieved from https://www.forbes.com/sites/forbescommunicationscouncil/2018/07/26/how-b2b-and-b2c-marketing-are-converging-today/#39f0bfdc54ce.

Bergstrom, B. (2018, June 21). 50 Social Media Best Practices Every Business Should Follow. Coschedule. Retrieved from https://coschedule.com/blog/social-media-best-practices-for-business/

Brandwatch analysis of 26,000 tweets. Retrieved from https://oursocialtimes.com/wp-content/uploads/2013/02/social-media-crisis-HSBC.jpg

Chi, C. (2021, Jan. 28). When Is the Best Time to Post on Instagram in 2021? Sourced from Sprout Social [Cheat Sheet]. Hubspot. Retrieved from https://blog.hubspot.com/marketing/instagram-best-time-post

Cvety. (2019, Sept. 20). 37 Mind Blowing YouTube Facts, Figures and Statistics – 2019. MerchDope. Retrieved from https://merchdope.com/youtube-stats/

DiSilvestro, A. (2016, Sept. 19). Yelp vs. Google vs. Facebook Reviews: which should you focus on and why? Search Engine Watch. Retrieved from https://searchenginewatch.com/2016/09/19/yelp-vs-Google-vs-facebook-reviews-which-should-you-focus-on-and-why/

Hannon, E. (2017. Feb 12). The Department of Education Misspells W.E.B. Du Bois' Name in Black History Month Tribute. Slate. Retrieved from https://slate.com/news-and-politics/2017/02/department-of-education-tweet-misspells-w-e-b-du-bois-name.html

Kircher, M. M. (2017, Feb 12). Department of Education Misspells Tweet About W.E.B. Du Bois, Also Misspells Its Apology Tweet. Intelligencer. Retrieved from http://nymag.com/intelligencer/2017/02/department-of-education-misspells-tweet.html

Little, J. (2015, March 24). Who Do You Trust? 92% of Consumers Trust Peer Recommendations Over Advertising. LinkedIn. Retrieved from https://www.linkedin.com/pulse/who-do-you-trust-92-consumers-peer-recommendations-over-joey-little/

McCaskill, A. (2015, Sept. 28). Recommendations From Friends Remain Most Credible Form of Advertising Among Consumers; Branded Websites Are the Second-Highest-Rated Form. Nielsen. Retrieved from https://www.nielsen.com/us/en/press-room/2015/recommendations-from-friends-remain-most-credible-form-of-advertising.html

Appendix

Petrescu, P. (2014, Oct. 1). Google Organic Click-Through Rates in 2014. Moz. Retreived from https://moz.com/blog/google-organic-click-through-rates-in-2014

Shesgreen, D. (2017, Feb 12). Education Dept. torched for misspelling W.E.B. Du Bois in tweet. USA Today. Retrieved from https://www.usatoday.com/story/news/politics/onpolitics/2017/02/12/education-dept-torched-tweet-misspells-du-bois-name/97820482/

Weidert Group (2021, February). B2B Video Statistics for 2021 from https://www.weidert.com/blog/b2b-video-marketing-statistics%3fhs_amp=true

2021, February, Instagram: distribution of global audiences 2021, by age group. Statista. com/statistics/325587/instagram-global-age-group/

Notes

Notes

About the author:

Chris Rosica
President, Rosica Communications
Author of *The Authentic Brand* and
The Business of Cause Marketing

Chris Rosica, president of Rosica Communications, is a recognized public relations and marketing expert, speaker, and author. He is passionate about integrated marketing and helping his clients grow, adapt to change, andoutpace the competition, and improve internal and external communications. Rosica's national PR firm was rated by Forbes in 2021 as one of "America's Best PR Agencies." His company specializes in B2B PR and social media, and primarily focuses in the areas of education, healthcare, nonprofit, food and beverage, and social impact. Rosica offers such thought leadership services as social media marketing, media relations, content development, crisis communications,brand positioning and messaging, issues management, and digital marketing (SEO/SEM). An authority on cause marketing, Rosica also authored *The Business of Cause Marketing: How Doing Good Means Doing Well* (Noble Press), which details the process and effects of incorporating cause marketing into a company's business and promotional agenda. He is a frequent keynote speaker, media trainer, and public speaking coach who coaches CEOs, salespeople, and corporate and nonprofit executives. Rosica has lectured at

Fordham University, Seton Hall, and PACE universities. As part of a symposium for the Young Presidents' Organization (YPO) and the Entrepreneurs' Organization (EO), Rosica received high accolades for his interview with renowned CEO Jack Welch. He is past president of New York City's chapter of Young Entrepreneurs' Organization (YEO or EO), and serves on several nonprofit boards, including Boys & Girls Clubs in New Jersey. Rosica graduated from the Entrepreneurial Master's program at MIT, is a graduate of Florida International and Johnson & Wales Universities and lives in New Jersey (and Vermont) with his wife, Wendy, daughter, and son.

The Authentic Brand
By Christopher Rosica

"A wonderful, increasingly enjoyable book."

—Michael Gerber
Author, The E-Myth Books

This book will change the way you think about how you brand yourself, your company and its products or services. Filled with personal stories and real-world experience from twelve top entrepreneurs, you will learn how these successful CEOs build their brands, balance work and family, find great employees, confront failures, and capitalize on their strengths.

"In the future, I think 'authenticity' will become a tremendously important concept for marketers. It's a great book."
—Al Ries—*Chairman, Ries & Ries, Author*

"The Authentic Brand gets to the heart of how companies connect with their customers by speaking to them at their level, never talking down to them. It's smart business and marketing for today's smart consumer culture."
—Jerry Greenfield—*Co-Founder, Ben & Jerry's Homemade*

Made in the USA
Middletown, DE
13 November 2021